What If We Do
NOTHING?

AIDS
AND OTHER EPIDEMICS

Carol Ballard

Gareth Stevens
Publishing

Please visit our web site at: www.garethstevens.com.
For a free color catalog describing Gareth Stevens Publishing's list of high-quality books, call 1-800-542-2595 (USA) or 1-800-387-3178 (Canada). Gareth Stevens Publishing's fax: 1-877-542-2596

Library of Congress Cataloging-in-Publication Data

Ballard, Carol.
    AIDS and other epidemics / by Carol Ballard.
      p. cm. – (What if we do nothing?)
    Includes bibliographical references and index.
    ISBN-10: 1-4339-0085-8   ISBN-13: 978-1-4339-0085-3 (lib. bdg.)
    1. AIDS (Disease) 2. Epidemics. 3. Communicable diseases. I. Title.
RA643.8.B354   2008
614.5'99392–dc22   2008029189

This North American edition published in 2009 by Gareth Stevens Publishing under license from Arcturus Publishing Limited.
Gareth Stevens Publishing
A Weekly Reader® Company
1 Reader's Digest Road
Pleasantville, NY 10570-7000 USA

Copyright © 2009 by Arcturus Publishing Limited
Produced by Arcturus Publishing Limited
26/27 Bickels Yard, 151-153 Bermondsey Street, London SE1 3HA

Gareth Stevens Managing Editor: Lisa M. Herrington
Gareth Stevens Editor: Jayne Keedle
Gareth Stevens Creative Director: Lisa Donovan

Series concept: Alex Woolf
Editor: Alex Woolf
Designer: Phipps Design
Picture researcher: Alex Woolf

Picture Credits: Corbis: Cover bottom left (Gideon Mendel), cover top right (Erik de Castro), 5 (Jose L Pelaez), 7 (Stefano Bianchetti), 12 (Gideon Mendel), 14 (Bettmann), 18 (Karen Kasmauski), 23 (Reuters), 24 (Reuters), 26 (Visuals Unlimited), 34 (CDC/PHIL), 36 (Louise Gubb), 43 (CDC/PHIL), 45 (Karen Kasmauski). Getty Images: 11 (MPI/Stringer), 17 (Robert Giroux), 40 (Andrew Caballero-Reynolds). Science Photo Library: Cover background (Mehau Kulyk), 9 (NIBSC), 28 (AJ Photo/Hop American), 30 (London School of Hygiene and Tropical Medicine), 32 (Philippepsaila), 39 (Paul Whitehill).

Cover pictures: Bottom left: A young South African woman with HIV.
Top right: People in Manila, Philippines, light candles to mark World AIDS Day.
Background: An illustration of HIV particles.

Every attempt has been made to clear copyright. Should there be any inadvertent omission, please apply to the publisher for rectification.

Printed in China

1 2 3 4 5 6 7 8 9 14 13 12 11 10 09 08

Contents

CHAPTER 1

Epidemic!

It is 2025. Emergency workers are practicing their response to a major breakout of an infectious disease. Health workers, police, and even the military are involved. Health workers are distributing vaccines to protect key workers. They are also practicing diagnosing cases of the disease and deciding who needs to go to the hospital. The police and army are enforcing quarantine areas to prevent the disease from spreading. Borders, ports, and airports are being patrolled to prevent more people who may be infected with disease from arriving from other countries. Luckily, it is all just practice. It is only a matter of time, however, before it could be for real.

What Are Infectious Diseases?

Infectious diseases are illnesses that can pass from one person to another, such as chickenpox, influenza, and meningitis. Under normal conditions, only a few people in a population tend to suffer from a particular infectious disease. A localized outbreak occurs when the number of cases of the disease increases rapidly within a small area. If the disease spreads more widely, affecting people over a larger area or a country, the outbreak is called an epidemic. If an outbreak spreads over an even larger area, covering several countries, a continent, or in the worst cases, the whole world, it is called a pandemic.

What Causes Infectious Diseases?

Infectious diseases are caused by microorganisms, or germs. These tiny life-forms are too small to see with the naked eye. They include bacteria, viruses, fungi, and parasites. There are several ways in which infectious diseases can spread from one person to another.

DETECTING AND MONITORING EPIDEMICS

The sooner an outbreak of an infectious disease is detected, the sooner action can be taken to minimize its spread. Satellites from the National Aeronautics and Space Administration (NASA) orbit Earth and collect global environmental data daily. This information is passed on to scientists who use it to help them track and predict outbreaks of disease. Early warnings give health organizations and governments additional time to respond to an outbreak and take immediate action.

How Do Infectious Diseases Spread?

■ **By air** When you cough or sneeze, air and droplets of liquid are expelled from your body very quickly. Germs spread into the air around you and can then be breathed in by anybody who is close.

■ **By water** Some germs thrive in dirty water. They enter the body when someone drinks the dirty water, or uses it for cooking.

■ **By food** Good storage keeps food free from disease-causing microorganisms. Cooking food kills any microorganisms that happen to be present in it. Poor hygiene and inadequate cooking can enable microorganisms to multiply in the food and infect anyone who eats it.

■ **By direct contact** Some infectious diseases are spread by direct contact with someone who is already infected. This might be by touch, or by the mixing of body fluids such as saliva and blood.

■ **By insects and other animals** Insects and other animals can also spread infections. For example, some disease-causing microorganisms are spread when an infected insect bites a person. A living thing that transmits an infection between individuals of another species is called a vector.

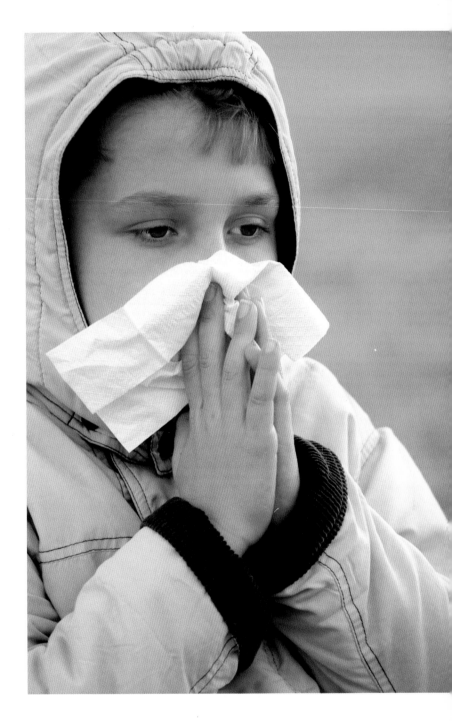

This boy has a cold. By using a tissue when he sneezes, he can reduce the chances of passing the infection to other people.

Fighting Infections

Your body has a natural defense mechanism. It is called your immune system. When your body encounters a disease-causing microorganism such as a virus or bacterium for the first time, your immune system makes chemicals called antibodies to help fight the infection. The process of fighting the infection takes a little time, during which you will probably be ill. The next time the same microorganism enters your body, however, your immune system is prepared. It recognizes the microorganism and responds swiftly so that you do not become ill. You are said to be immune to the infection.

Why Do Epidemics Occur?

Most people have experienced a localized outbreak of a particular infection, such as an upset stomach. An outbreak begins with a few cases. In a short time, a large number of people within a small area are infected. Then the outbreak slowly dies away. An epidemic arises when the number of infected cases does not die away but increases. In such situations, the outbreak expands.

Epidemics can arise for a variety of reasons. Within any population, a proportion of people will be immune to an infectious disease. The infection does not affect everybody. However, many viruses and bacteria can change, or mutate, giving rise to new types. When this happens, even fewer people will be immune to the new type. The infection will affect a large number of people and spread rapidly over a wider area — an epidemic occurs.

Another way an epidemic can occur is if an infectious disease that is common in one part of the world is taken to another part of the world. The people there will not have been exposed to that infection before and so nobody will be immune to it. This has happened in the past, with infections being carried by traders, armies, and explorers as they moved from country to country. When Europeans came to the Americas, they brought smallpox, a highly contagious disease, to the continent. Scientists estimate that smallpox may have killed 20 million people, or 95 percent of the native population.

VACCINES AND VACCINATION

Vaccination is a way of creating immunity to an infection. To do this, a substance called a vaccine is given to the patient, either by mouth or injection. The vaccine contains dead or weakened viruses and bacteria. These cannot cause an infection, but they stimulate the immune system in the same way that the live microorganisms would. This means that if the person encounters the live microorganisms in the future, his or her immune system would respond quickly, preventing an infection from occurring.

Environmental Effects

Infectious diseases, especially those that are spread by dirty water, can often reach epidemic proportions. This is especially true in developing countries where large numbers of people live in cramped conditions with poor sanitation. This is also the situation in many refugee camps.

Modern Travel

In the modern world, global air travel enables the spread of germs over great distances. Epidemics can occur rapidly, becoming pandemics as they spread across large areas of the world.

Many people died during a cholera epidemic in Paris, France, in 1832. The filthy living conditions shown in the picture were probably partly to blame.

WHAT WOULD YOU DO?

You Are in Charge

As a medical advisor to the government you have been asked to develop a way to detect epidemics early. To do that, you need information. Which of the following would be most helpful to enable the earliest possible detection? Why?

■ Ask doctors to report the number of cases of infectious diseases that they diagnose each week.

■ Keep a map showing the location of every reported case and how those cases are spread.

■ Create a database containing information about each person infected, including their age, gender, ethnic group, and recent history of foreign travels.

CHAPTER 2

HIV/AIDS

It is 2025. The HIV/AIDS crisis has reached a critical level in many countries. People all around the world are infected. Millions of people have died from the disease and many more are very ill. Large numbers of children are orphaned. Resources are stretched thin as governments and aid agencies struggle to look after them all properly. Governments and health groups are organizing campaigns to tell people about HIV/AIDS and the steps each individual can take to guard against infection. Scientists are searching desperately to find a cure for HIV/AIDS. Others are trying to develop a vaccine to protect people against infection. Medicines are available to treat the illness but they are so expensive that many people cannot afford them.

What Is HIV/AIDS?

AIDS stands for Acquired Immune Deficiency Syndrome. When the first cases were reported in the United States in 1981, nobody understood what caused the disease. In 1983, scientists in France and the United States identified a virus they called Human Immunodeficiency Virus (HIV) as the cause of AIDS. Two years later, blood tests to detect the presence of HIV in patients were developed. People who are infected with HIV are said to be HIV positive.

Where Did HIV/AIDS Come From?

Many infectious diseases have been known about for hundreds of years. HIV/AIDS, however, appeared to be a completely new disease. Most scientists believe HIV/AIDS originated in Sub-Saharan Africa. Many believe that the disease first appeared in monkeys and then crossed over into humans. From there, it spread rapidly throughout Sub-Saharan Africa and to the rest of the world.

Effects of HIV/AIDS

The body's immune system protects people from infections and other diseases. HIV attacks and destroys the immune system, so the person's defenses against other infections and diseases are weakened. Therefore, people with HIV become ill with many diseases that a healthy immune system would ward off. People can remain HIV positive for many years. Eventually, however, the illness progresses to its final stage, which is called AIDS. The person with AIDS becomes increasingly ill from infections and other complications such as cancer or pneumonia, which ultimately causes his or her death.

Diagnosing HIV/AIDS

Infection with HIV can be diagnosed by testing for antibodies in a sample of blood, urine, or saliva. However, as there can be a delay of several months between infection and the appearance of the antibodies, this test is not always ideal. A more immediate diagnosis can be made by testing for chemicals of HIV particles.

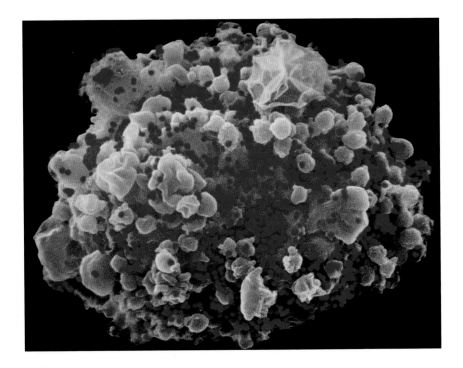

The white blood cell in this micrograph (a photo of an image seen through a microscope) is infected with HIV, seen here as red dots. The virus kills the white blood cells, weakening the immune system.

What Are the Symptoms of HIV/AIDS?

People who are infected with HIV suffer from repeated infections, especially colds, coughs, and chest infections. In later stages, diarrhea also becomes common. Fevers, chills, weakness, and weight loss, together with infections and tumors, are characteristic of the final stages of AIDS.

How Does HIV/AIDS Spread?

HIV/AIDS is not spread by regular, daily contact with an HIV-positive person. You can't get HIV/AIDS by hugging a person. It's not spread through the air, like a cold. For a healthy person to become infected with HIV, the person's body fluids must mix with body fluids from a person who has the virus. There are several ways this can happen:

- **Sexual contact** In most cases of HIV infection, the infection is spread by sexual contact. That can be avoided by sexual abstinence, or by practicing safe sex.
- **Exposure to HIV-positive blood** In the early days of AIDS, people who received blood transfusions sometimes became infected with HIV. Then scientists learned more about the virus and how it was transmitted. Today, in developed countries, HIV infection from blood and blood products is rare. Blood is routinely screened before it is used to make sure it is not HIV positive. In many developing countries, however, blood is not screened for HIV. In those countries, HIV infections are still spread by contaminated blood.
- **Mother-to-child contact** HIV can pass from mother to child during the last weeks of pregnancy, or during a normal birth. The risk can be greatly reduced if the mother is given drug treatment during pregnancy, and if the baby is born by cesarean section.
- **Other routes** Health workers exposed to HIV-infected blood take many safety precautions. However, they are still at risk if the virus enters their body. An infected needle, for instance, might accidentally pierce their skin through the rubber gloves they wear. Without proper safety precautions, tattooing and body piercing also pose a risk if needles become contaminated with infected blood. Drug addicts who share needles also have a higher-than-normal risk of HIV infection.

Who Does HIV/AIDS Affect?

HIV/AIDS affects a wide variety of people. It cuts across race, age, gender, social, and geographic boundaries. The disease infects men and women around the world in equal numbers. It also infects children of all ages. Each year, the number of people infected with HIV increases.

RYAN WHITE

In 1984, a boy named Ryan White contracted HIV/AIDS after receiving a transfusion of HIV-infected blood. At the time, little was known about HIV/AIDS and how it spread. Many people were afraid of getting the disease. Ryan, then 13, was banned from his school. He and his family were shunned by the community in his hometown of Kokomo, Indiana. People were so hostile that his family decided to move to Cicero, Indiana. Ryan's experience with HIV/AIDS and the way he and his family had been treated drew national media attention. Ryan became a spokesperson for people with HIV/AIDS. He campaigned for people to treat them fairly and with dignity. Ryan died in 1990 at the age of 18. Later that year, Congress passed the Ryan White Comprehensive AIDS Resources Emergency (CARE) Act, which ensures financial support for people living with HIV/AIDS. Sadly, many people still do not know all the facts about HIV/AIDS. In many places, people with the disease and their families are still treated like outcasts.

In 2007, UNAIDS and the World Health Organization (WHO) reported that 33.2 million people around the world were living with HIV. That figure included 2.5 million children under the age of 15. That year, about 2.5 million people were newly infected with the virus. Another 2.1 million people died of AIDS.

Sub-Saharan Africa has been hardest hit by the epidemic. Nearly two-thirds of all HIV-infected people live in that region. About 61 percent of all adults infected there are women.

If we do nothing, some people think that by 2025, the death toll from AIDS in Africa alone since 1980 could add up to 60 million adults and 15 million children. As many as 22.4 million African children could be orphaned.

After Ryan White was diagnosed with HIV/AIDS, he had to fight a long legal battle to be allowed to continue attending school. His campaign turned him into a national celebrity and spokesperson for AIDS awareness.

Treating HIV/AIDS

Medicines are available to treat people diagnosed with HIV. However, these medicines only slow the progression of the illness. There is as yet no known cure.

A common approach to treating HIV/AIDS is known as HAART (highly active antiretroviral therapy). Patients take a mixture of several drugs to stabilize their symptoms and to reduce the amount of virus in their body. This can improve their general health and increase their survival time. However, not all patients are able to stay on the HAART treatment. Some experience unpleasant side effects, while others find the process too complicated.

Antiretroviral drugs are very expensive and need to be taken for the rest of a person's life. Many HIV/AIDS patients can't afford the drugs, especially in developing countries where they are desperately needed.

New Drugs

Researchers are trying to develop new, more effective drugs to treat HIV/AIDS. Recent advances in the science of genetics have helped. A gene is a tiny unit of a plant or animal cell. Genes determine the characteristics that are passed from parent to offspring. Some

A healthcare worker explains the HIV test to children before she tests them. Their mother is HIV positive, but the tests showed that none of the children were infected.

researchers are hoping to develop a drug that will work on the HIV gene that would stop the virus from multiplying. The person would still be infected but since the virus could not multiply, the person would not become ill.

Preventing Infection

Many countries have introduced education programs to inform people about HIV/AIDS. These programs aim to prevent the spread of HIV by teaching people how to avoid infection. Such programs stress the importance of sexual abstinence, staying with only one partner, and practicing safe sex. It is far easier to prevent the spread of HIV than it is to treat AIDS.

Search for a Vaccine

Vaccines help the body's immune system fight off specific diseases. As every microorganism is different, however, a vaccine can only offer protection against a single microorganism. Scientists are trying to develop a vaccine that will offer protection against HIV. The problem is that, like most viruses, HIV does not stay the same. It changes over time. That makes it difficult to create a vaccine, because it has to be altered to match the new version of the virus.

WHAT WOULD YOU DO?

You Are in Charge

You are a health official in a country with an increasing number of HIV/AIDS cases. You have limited funding. What percentage of your total budget do you spend on...

- trying to reduce the number of new cases by educating the general public about how to avoid infection?
- buying drugs to treat people who are already ill to keep them healthier for longer periods?
- scientific research to develop a vaccine to prevent new HIV cases from occurring?

Which option would be immediately effective in controlling the spread of HIV/AIDS? Which option or options hold the most promise for controlling the disease in the future?

CHAPTER 3

Influenza

It is 2025. The world is in the grip of a global influenza pandemic. International travel is restricted. Within individual countries, travel restrictions and quarantine zones are in force. Hospitals are overwhelmed. Many people who need hospital treatment have to stay at home. Drugs for treating the sick are running out. Factories and schools are closed. Movie theaters, restaurants, sports arenas, and other places where large numbers of people gather are also closed. Graves cannot be dug quickly enough to bury the dead. Food supplies are running low. Other vital services such as water and electricity are failing. People are scared and governments seem powerless to improve the situation.

Could Influenza Really Be That Bad?

Most people think of influenza — or flu, as it is usually called — as a very bad cold. Influenza can be deadly, though, especially for young children and the elderly. In a normal year, ten to twenty percent of the population of the United States will suffer from influenza. About 36,000 people will die from complications. In a major epidemic, those figures would be much higher.

Volunteers in Cincinnati, Ohio, feed the children of families struck down by the 1918-1919 influenza pandemic. Many people wore face masks to try to avoid becoming infected.

Influenza Pandemic of 1918-1919

In March 1918, during World War I, an influenza outbreak began in an army camp in Kansas. Another outbreak began in Europe around the same time. No one knows for sure where the flu originated but research suggests it may have come from Asia. Soldiers from the United States and Europe carried the infection with them, helping it to spread rapidly. By August, the epidemic

was gaining strength. Influenza became a worldwide pandemic during the winter of 1918 and 1919. Unlike most flu viruses, this one killed not just children and the elderly, but also healthy people in their 20s and 30s. It is estimated that more than 20 percent of the world's population became ill during the outbreak. Between 2.5 percent and 5 percent of them died, or more than 50 million people.

Learning From the Past

If the same proportion of today's global population of 6.7 billion were to become affected by an influenza pandemic, more than 1.3 billion people would become ill. Between 165 million and 300 million people would die. Luckily, though, we can learn lessons from the past. The World Health Organization (WHO) and other agencies monitor outbreaks of many different infections, including influenza. Governments have plans that can be put into action fast if an epidemic begins. Some supplies of vaccine are available to protect key workers, such as medical staff and those involved in maintaining vital services. More doses of vaccine could be produced in a relatively short time for other people. Health experts hope that if another major epidemic were to break out, those measures would help authorities stop its spread and reduce its impact.

This map shows the World Health Organization's surveillance network of laboratories that monitor the world for outbreaks of influenza epidemics. The countries in red have a national network of laboratories. The orange countries have more than one laboratory, and the yellow countries have just one WHO laboratory. The blue countries have no laboratories.

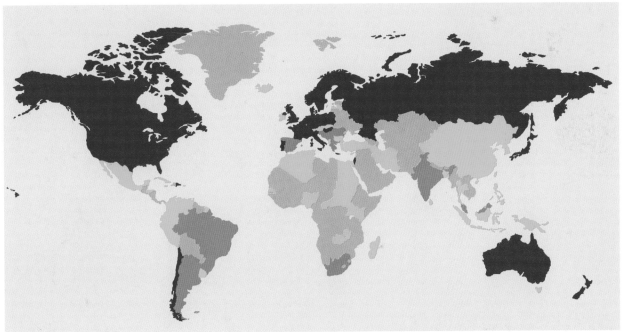

Source: www.brown.edu/Courses/Bio_160/Projects1999/flu/epidemiology.html

What Causes Influenza?

Influenza is caused by influenza viruses. There are many different influenza viruses but they fall into three categories, known as types A, B, and C. Types A and B can cause influenza epidemics. Type C usually only causes mild cases of flu. The outer coat of each influenza virus contains two proteins, known as H and N. Each protein can exist in several different forms. Each form is given a number, such as H1 or H2. The combination of different H and N forms is used to identify the influenza strains. For example, the virus responsible for the 1918–1919 pandemic was the H1N1 strain.

New Strains

Like other viruses, an influenza virus can mutate over time. That creates new strains of the virus that are similar to the original but different in some ways. An influenza epidemic is usually caused by a virus strain that has not been seen before. Because very few people in the population will be immune to the new strain, infection rates will be very high. If the same strain appears a second time, the outbreak will be much less serious. That's because people's previous exposure to the virus will have caused their immune systems to produce antibodies to fight it.

TIME LINE OF INFLUENZA EPIDEMICS, 1918-2004

This time line shows some of the major influenza epidemics and pandemics that occurred during the 20th and early 21st centuries.

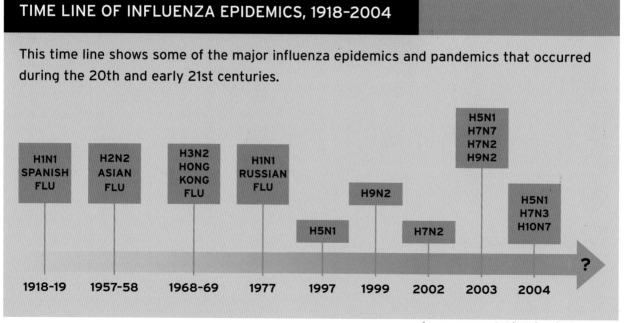

Source: www.news.cornell.edu/stories/Oct05/Avian_Torres.kr.html

What Are the Symptoms of Influenza?

Influenza viruses cause a variety of symptoms. The most common symptoms are shivering and body aches, headaches, coughing, and chest pains. A fever develops rapidly and lasts for several days. During and afterward, a patient often feels tired and weak for a week or more.

Influenza infections are typically more serious in the elderly and in young children. Complications such as chest infections often follow a bout of influenza. Those aren't caused by the flu virus but by other infections picked up while the body was weakened.

How Is Influenza Treated?

Some antiviral drugs can be used to treat influenza. In most cases, however, doctors allow the infection to run its course. The patient's own immune system will usually overcome it. Most medicines sold as flu remedies are designed only to treat flu symptoms. They cannot cure the infection.

Vaccination

Vaccines provide some protection from influenza. In some countries those are made available every year to the elderly, to children, and to people with medical conditions, such as asthma, for whom influenza would be most serious. However, vaccine makers can only estimate which of the many strains of influenza will be the next to emerge. If an unexpected strain of the virus causes an outbreak, they have to rush to make a specific vaccine to fight it. The protection offered by an influenza vaccine is not long-lived, so many people have an annual vaccination each fall.

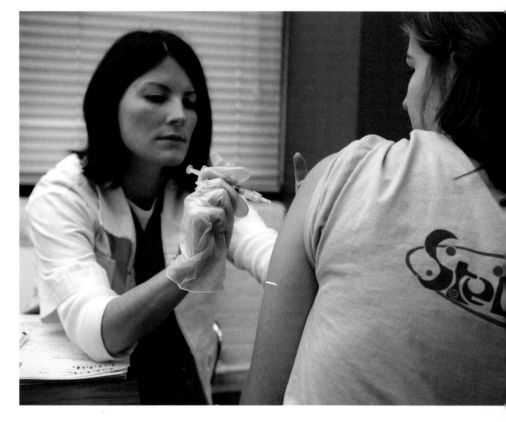

Like this girl, many people in the developed world are now regularly vaccinated against influenza.

A girl herds ducks through pig pens in a village in China. The chance of an influenza infection passing from species to species increases in crowded conditions like these.

Avian Influenza

In recent years, there have been numerous news reports about outbreaks of avian influenza, or bird flu. Some experts have predicted that a bird flu pandemic is very likely in the near future. But what is bird flu and why are some people so worried about it?

Avian influenza is a type of influenza that affects birds, hence its common name. Wild birds carry the virus in their bodies but it does not usually make them ill. However, wild bird carriers can pass the disease on via body fluids and waste to domesticated birds such as chickens, turkeys, and ducks. The infection makes these birds very ill and, in many cases, they die. Bird flu can spread rapidly through poultry flocks, with devastating effects.

Which Viruses Are Involved?

The viruses responsible for bird flu are type A influenza viruses. There are different strains influenza viruses, each with a particular combination of H and N proteins in its coat, just like the viruses that cause human influenza.

18

How Can Birds Infect Humans?

Avian influenza viruses can infect humans. However, only people who have been in very close contact with infected birds usually get sick. Symptoms in humans include fever, cough, aches, and breathing difficulties. It is very rare for avian influenza to be passed from one person to another.

Why the Flap About Bird Flu?

One strain of avian influenza virus, called H5N1, is known to spread very quickly among birds and to have a high mortality (death) rate. H5N1 does not usually infect people, but when it does, it is very dangerous. The H5N1 form of avian influenza is sometimes fatal, even in healthy people. It is a strain that mutates rapidly. People worry that the virus could mutate in humans in a way that makes it easier to spread from person to person.

When a virus infects a person or animal, it reproduces rapidly. If the person or animal is infected by two different viruses at the same time, the combination can create a new virus. This new virus will have some characteristics of each of the original viruses.

The transition from an infection in wild birds to an infection that passes rapidly from person to person would have several stages (see the diagram on the right). Scientists are worried that this sequence of events could result in a highly infectious and very dangerous form of influenza virus. That strain could cause an epidemic or even a pandemic. Although H5N1 seems to be the virus strain that is most likely to mutate, other strains that are being monitored include H7N1 and H9N2.

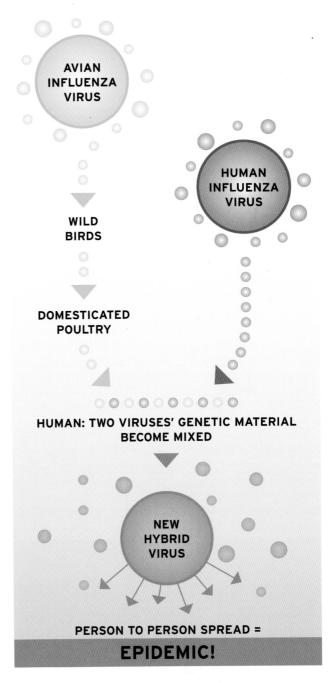

This diagram illustrates how a new hybrid (crossbred or mixed) virus could arise from the combination of an avian influenza virus and a human influenza virus.

AVIAN INFLUENZA VIRUS

HUMAN INFLUENZA VIRUS

WILD BIRDS

DOMESTICATED POULTRY

HUMAN: TWO VIRUSES' GENETIC MATERIAL BECOME MIXED

NEW HYBRID VIRUS

PERSON TO PERSON SPREAD =

EPIDEMIC!

GLOBAL RISK OF AVIAN INFLUENZA OUTBREAKS, 2003-2008

Endemic Risk Some cases occurring all the time among both people and animals

Epidemic Risk Some occasional outbreaks in animals

High Risk Near to countries with human or animal cases, or at risk from bird migration and/or transport

At Risk Bird migration and/or transport may lead to animal cases

Pandemic Risk Animal cases are unlikely, but region would be affected by a human pandemic

Source: www.usaid.gov/our_work/global_health/home/News/news_items/avian_influenza.html

Human Cases of Bird Flu

The World Health Organization (WHO) tracks cases of bird flu in people. The number of H5N1 infections appears to be increasing.

This world map shows the risk posed to each country by avian influenza.

- **1997** Several hundred people became infected with the H5N1 virus in Hong Kong and six people died. To prevent the spread of this virus, all the chickens in Hong Kong were killed.
- **2004** Forty-six infections of H5N1 were reported in Thailand and Vietnam, resulting in 32 deaths.
- **2005** Ninety-eight cases of H5N1 infections were confirmed in Vietnam, Thailand, China, Cambodia, and Indonesia, resulting in 43 deaths.
- **2006** There were 115 cases of H5N1 infections confirmed in nine countries in Asia and the Middle East, resulting in 79 deaths.
- **2007** Nine countries, including two in Africa, reported a total of 88 cases of H5N1 flu, resulting in 59 deaths.

Minimizing the Risk of a Bird Flu Epidemic

Governments and international organizations are aware of the potential risk of a bird flu epidemic in humans. Several plans are in place to minimize that risk. They include the following precautions:

- **Monitoring wild and domesticated birds worldwide** Wild birds are monitored, especially along migration routes. Any domesticated birds found to be infected are culled (killed) along with the rest of the flock to which they belong. Farms, nature reserves, and other areas can be quarantined. Farmers are ordered to bring domesticated poultry indoors if the birds are at risk.
- **Global reporting and information exchange** Sharing information means quick and appropriate actions can be taken.
- **Vaccination** Birds close to an outbreak may be vaccinated in an attempt to prevent the spread of the infection.
- **Changing farming methods** Close contact between birds and people has been reduced wherever possible. However, many poor rural communities find it hard to change traditional lifestyles, with birds and people living closely together. A bird flu epidemic in humans is therefore more likely to appear in a rural area.
- **Improving veterinary services** Having qualified and experienced veterinary doctors increases the chance of containing a bird flu outbreak quickly and efficiently.

If an Epidemic Begins...

There are plans in place in case an outbreak of bird flu begins to spread from person to person. These include distributing antiviral drugs to people at risk. Most countries have stockpiled vaccine, while many others have the ability to produce large amounts of vaccine quickly. Sharing information between countries could reduce the time it takes to identify the virus and develop a vaccine.

WHAT WOULD YOU DO?

You Are in Charge

There is a major outbreak of avian influenza in humans and vaccine supplies are limited. As the government official responsible for health, do you order medical staff to:

- vaccinate as many people as possible - first come, first served?
- vaccinate anybody who can afford to pay?
- vaccinate only healthcare workers?
- vaccinate only the most vulnerable people?

Which approach do you think would be the most effective way to use your vaccine stocks? Why?

CHAPTER 4

SARS

It is 2025. An outbreak of severe acute respiratory syndrome (SARS) has been confirmed. The number of people infected is increasing daily. SARS has now reached epidemic levels. The first cluster of cases occurred in a small area. Now, new cases are appearing in different countries every day. People around the world are worried that they might catch SARS. In the worst-hit regions, hospitals do not have enough quarantine areas to isolate all the SARS patients. This makes it harder to stop the disease from spreading. People are being urged not to travel abroad. People living in affected areas are wearing face masks when they go outside. All students have been instructed to wear masks in school. Governments are worried that it is just a matter of time before the outbreak becomes a global pandemic.

What Is SARS?

Severe acute respiratory syndrome (SARS) was the first new disease to appear in the 21st century. Symptoms usually appear within two to ten days of infection. Patients have a high fever, aches and discomfort, and a dry cough that makes breathing difficult. SARS is caused by a coronavirus. Viewed under a microscope, the virus looks like a crown, or corona. This is the same type of virus that causes the common cold and pneumonia. The coronavirus that causes SARS is called SARS-CoV. Research in China suggested that the virus originated in horseshoe bats and spread to humans via wild civet cats. Neither the bats nor the cats showed any signs of the illness.

The First Outbreak

In November 2002, a farmer in Guangdong Province in China was diagnosed with an unusual type of lung infection. The patient died soon afterward. A doctor became infected, too. He then traveled to Hong Kong, carrying the disease with him. From there, the disease spread quickly in Asia and then to North America, Europe, and eventually worldwide.

Delayed Reaction

The Chinese authorities delayed reporting the initial outbreak in China to the World Health Organization. For that reason, emergency measures were not taken in the early stages of the outbreak. By the time government health organizations reacted, the disease had spread too far to be easily contained. Some of the ways people tried to restrict the spread of SARS included:

- setting up a worldwide communications network for medical workers to exchange information
- extensive use of quarantine
- screening airline passengers for SARS symptoms
- using isolation hospitals to treat SARS patients

These students and their teacher in Hong Kong are wearing masks to protect themselves from catching severe acute respiratory syndrome (SARS). Similar precautions were taken in many workplaces.

Who Was Affected?

At the start of the outbreak, few people understood the risks posed by SARS. Many medical workers were infected in the early days, until people realized that SARS patients posed a risk to them too and that all SARS patients needed to be isolated. Worldwide, more than 8,000 people became ill with SARS in 2003. Of those, 813 died. The illness was more severe in people over age 65 than in younger people.

SARS CASES AND DEATHS, 2003

	February	March	April	May	June	July
cases	167	1,455	4,041	2,697	87	0
deaths	4	54	314	392	47	2

A scientist performs tests on the SARS virus at a laboratory in China.

How Does SARS Spread?

SARS spreads from person to person via body fluids. It is usually transmitted by droplets of liquid that are dispersed into the air when a person coughs or sneezes. SARS can also be transmitted by sexual contact. The virus is contagious at every stage of the infection. This means that people can infect others even before they show any symptoms of the illness themselves. Patients are still infectious for ten days after the end of the fever.

How Is SARS Treated?

There is no effective treatment for SARS. In many cases, all medical staff can do is make patients more comfortable and try to ease their symptoms. Extra oxygen can help patients breathe easier. Research suggests that some of the worst SARS symptoms are caused by the body's immune system overreacting to the virus. Future treatments may involve drugs that limit the body's immune response.

Scientists have developed vaccines that are effective against the virus strain responsible for the 2003 SARS outbreak. The vaccines could be used to protect medical workers and others deemed to be at high risk in the event of another SARS outbreak. However, the vaccines may offer only limited protection against new strains of the SARS virus. Indeed, the current vaccines may not work at all if the virus has mutated.

Wiping Out SARS

In May 2005, the World Health Organization declared that SARS was contained. There had been no reports of new cases for more than a year. Now it is believed that the SARS virus exists only in secure laboratories. As long as it remains locked away, the virus should never reappear. However, it could arise again naturally, or someone could let the virus out of the laboratory by accident or on purpose.

WHAT WOULD YOU DO?

You Are in Charge

The SARS outbreak has not yet reached your country. As head of the government, you want to keep your country SARS-free. Do you:

- ban all travel into and out of the country, even though the ban could be disastrous for trade and could affect supplies of food and other essentials?

- ban travel only to and from areas known to have SARS cases, although the disease may have already spread to new areas?

- isolate people arriving in the country for a quarantine period, then allow them in, although this will stretch medical services to the limit?

- screen airline passengers arriving in the country for symptoms of SARS, although you know that symptoms rarely appear in the early stages of infection?

Which of those options do you think would be the best course of action? Why?

CHAPTER 5

Antibiotic-Resistant Infections

It is 2025. Illnesses that had once been controllable and posed little risk to human life are now deadly killers. Even a simple cut can lead to a life-threatening infection. This is because antibiotic drugs, once used to treat numerous illnesses and infections, no longer work. Infected patients are nursed in isolation to prevent the spread of disease. Many people are reluctant to go to the hospital for fear of catching something deadly. Any one of these infections could develop into an epidemic, in which there would be no effective medicine. Scientists are in a race against time to develop new antibiotics. When they do, though, the bacteria rapidly develop resistance to them, and so different antibiotics are needed.

What Are Antibiotic-Resistant Infections?

Most people have taken antibiotics at some point. These drugs are used to treat many bacterial infections. Some kill the bacteria. Others prevent them from reproducing. The first antibiotic available for use in patients was penicillin. It was introduced in the late 1940s. Doctors were delighted that at last they had an effective treatment for often-deadly bacterial infections. Before long, however, doctors began to notice that some bacteria had adapted to become resistant to penicillin.

As more antibiotics were developed during the 1950s and 1960s, their use increased rapidly. So, too, did the appearance of resistant strains of bacteria. For example, methicillin was introduced in 1960 to treat *Staphylococcus aureus* (MRSA) infections. The first strains of methicillin-resistant *Staphylococcus aureus* (MRSA) were reported within a few months.

The green dots in this micrograph are antibiotic-resistant *Staphylococcus aureus* cells. They are shown on the surface of the small intestine.

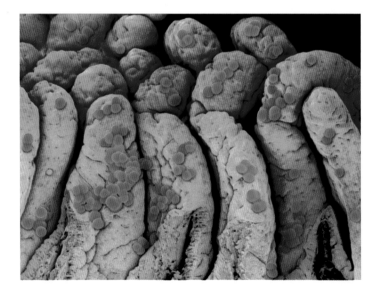

Resistant strains of other bacteria have also emerged. *Clostridium difficile (C. diff)*, which causes severe diarrhea, poses a special problem. Its spores can remain active for a long time, and until recently, there was no known way to kill them. A wide range of bacteria, including *Escherichia coli (E. Coli)*, which causes food poisoning, are also developing resistance to widely used antibiotics.

Like all living organisms, bacteria must evolve and adapt to survive. For many years, scientists have warned that over-using antibiotics could give rise to bacteria capable of resisting their beneficial effects. Indeed, as antibiotic use has continued, increasing numbers of bacterial-resistant strains have emerged.

People get antibiotic-resistant infections in one of two ways:
■ by catching an already existing antibiotic-resistant strain of bacteria
■ by developing a bacterial infection that changes in the body to become resistant to the antibiotic that is being used to treat it

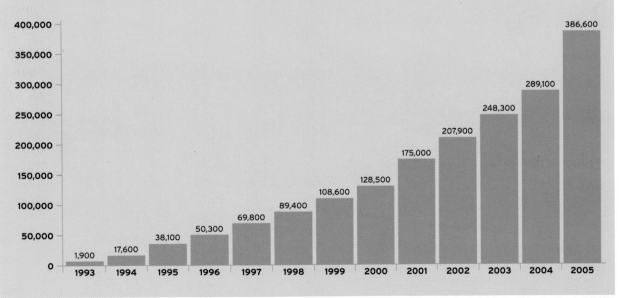

MRSA CASES IN U.S. HOSPITALS

This graph shows the dramatic increase in the number of MRSA cases in U.S. hospitals between 1993 and 2005. There were fewer than 2,000 cases in 1993, compared to nearly 400,000 cases in 2005.

Source: AHRQ, Center for Delivery, Organization, and Markets, Healthcare Cost and Utilization Project, Nationwide Inpatient Sample, 1993-2005

Preventing Infections

Hospitals are attempting to reduce the number of antibiotic-resistant infections by improving healthcare workers' hygiene. Many are testing all patients admitted to the hospital. Those with infections are isolated to prevent the spread of infection.

How Bacteria Becomes Resistant

Bacteria can develop resistance to antibiotics by interfering with the ways in which the antibiotics work. For example, penicillin kills bacteria by attaching itself to the bacterial cell wall. It destroys part of the wall and the bacterium dies. Bacteria can become resistant to this action in one of two ways:

- by altering their walls so that the penicillin cannot attach itself to them
- by using chemicals to dismantle the penicillin molecules

These changes occur in the genetic information of the bacterium, so the changes are maintained in all new bacteria that develop during the infection.

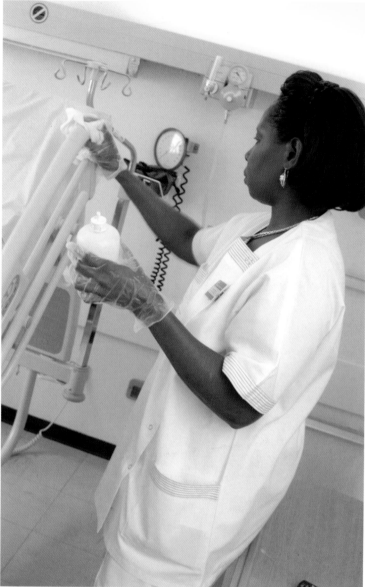

Thorough cleaning and disinfecting of hospital beds and equipment is essential. It reduces the spread of infection from patient to patient.

Antibiotic-Resistant Tuberculosis

Tuberculosis (TB) is a disease found in most countries of the world. In developing countries, it affects the lungs as well as other organs. In industrialized countries, it generally affects only the lungs.

TB is responsible for nearly two million deaths around the world every year. It is caused by a bacterium called *Mycobacterium tuberculosis*. It spreads when an infected person coughs or sneezes.

Since the introduction of antibiotics, it has been possible to treat TB effectively. However, in recent years doctors have found some strains of the bacterium that are resistant to antibiotics. Some are resistant to two or more of the antibiotics that would normally be a doctor's first choice for treating TB. These strains are known as multi-drug resistant TB, or MDR TB. Patients with MDR TB have to be treated with other drugs that are more expensive and have more severe side effects. In 2006, WHO estimated there were 425,000 cases of MDR TB globally each year. Even worse, strains of TB have now appeared that are resistant to all the first-choice drugs and more than six of the second-choice drugs. They are known as extreme drug resistant strains (XDR TB) and are virtually untreatable.

Teams of scientists are investigating the drug-resistant TB strains. They are researching how the bacterium becomes resistant to different drugs. They hope to develop new drugs that the TB bacterium won't be able to resist.

Out of the Hospitals

Antibiotic-resistant infections first affected only hospital patients. The immune systems of people who were already sick or weakened could not overcome the infections. Recently, though, some strains have been found in healthy people who did not catch them in hospitals. Cases of previously healthy people infected with drug-resistant strains of MRSA have now been reported in North America and in Europe. The possibility that such infections could reach epidemic levels is a cause for serious concern, as we would have no effective means to treat them.

WHAT WOULD YOU DO?

You Are in Charge

As a government health official, what steps would you take to reduce the incidence of antibiotic-resistant infections?

■ limit antibiotic use in humans

■ improve hospital hygiene

■ test everybody and quarantine anybody found to be carrying an antibiotic-resistant infection

■ research new antibiotics to which bacteria are not yet resistant

Which of these do you think would be most effective? Why?

CHAPTER 6

Viral Hemorrhagic Fevers

It is 2025. A fierce viral epidemic is raging throughout regions of Africa and the Middle East. Many people are sick and the death toll is rising. Authorities hope to limit the spread of the infection by clearing garbage dumps and other rat-infested places. Grain is being transferred to rodent-proof containers. Governments and aid agencies are telling people not to dispose of waste close to their homes. They are also being encouraged to maintain higher standards of hygiene. This, however, can be difficult in areas where sanitation is poor and the availability of water is limited.

What Are Viral Hemorrhagic Fevers?

There are many different viral hemorrhagic fevers (VHFs), including Ebola fever, Marburg fever, Lassa fever, and Rift Valley fever. Although each disease is caused by a different virus, there are some similarities between them. All VHFs usually affect many organs of the body at the same time and often cause internal bleeding. Symptoms include fever, tiredness, dizziness, aching muscles, weakness, and exhaustion. Although some only cause mild illnesses, others are usually fatal. Antiviral drugs sometimes help, but in many cases there is no effective treatment for these viruses.

Where Do VHFs Occur?

VHFs generally occur in tropical countries. Each virus has been known to occur within a limited geographic area. That is because the viruses depend on an animal or insect host and can only survive in areas where their host species lives. Humans are not the natural host

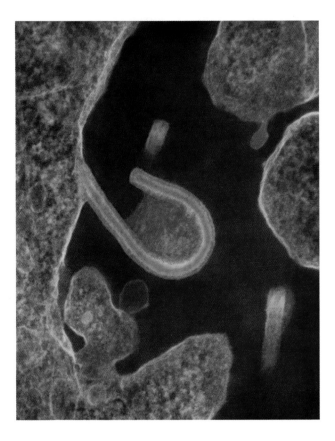

This micrograph shows the release of an Ebola virus (blue and green) from a host cell (green/pink). By taking part of the host cell with it, the virus is able to avoid the host's immune system.

for any of these viruses. Humans can become infected only after coming into contact with infected host animals or insects. Once a human is infected, though, he or she can pass the infection on to other humans.

People occasionally become infected by a host that is far from its native habitat. For example, in 1967, laboratory workers in Marburg, Germany, became infected by monkeys imported from Uganda, which were infected with a virus from that country. The virus was named Marburg virus. Also, a person who becomes infected in one place may travel elsewhere and infect other people in distant places. With the expansion of international travel, outbreaks of these diseases are appearing in countries where they have never been seen before.

How Do People Become Infected?

How people become infected with VHFs depends on the type of animal or insect that the virus uses as a host. For example, viruses carried by rodents are transmitted when humans come into contact with waste from infected animals. Viruses carried by insects are transmitted when an infected insect bites a human. This table shows examples of VHFs, their hosts, and the ways the viruses are transmitted to humans.

SOME VIRAL HEMORRHAGIC FEVERS

Infection	Host	Means of transmission
Ebola virus	unknown; research suggests a bat species	via body fluids such as blood, feces, and saliva of infected nonhuman primates (e.g. chimpanzee)
Marburg virus	unknown	uncertain, but possibly via infected non-human primates (e.g. apes and monkeys)
Lassa fever	multimammate rat	contact with infected rats or their waste
Dengue fever	mosquito	mosquito bite
Crimean-Congo fever	tick	tick infects livestock such as cattle, sheep, and goats. Humans are then infected via contact with blood or other infected tissues from livestock, or directly by a tick bite.
Rift Valley fever	blood-sucking sandflies	sandfly bite

Preventing Viral Hemorrhagic Infections

Vaccines are available that offer protection against yellow fever and Argentine hemorrhagic fever. As yet, however, no effective vaccines have been developed against the other VHFs. Currently, the only way to prevent infection is to avoid contact with the host species.

For diseases that are spread by rodents, the best ways to avoid infection are to control rodent populations, to discourage rodents from entering or living in homes and workplaces, and to encourage the safe clean-up of rodent nests and droppings. Diseases that are spread by insects, such as mosquitoes, may be prevented by using insecticide, insect repellent, clothing to cover the body so the skin is not exposed, mosquito nets, and window screens. Diseases that are spread by contact with nonhuman primates are best prevented by avoiding contact with infected primates.

Researchers in Ivory Coast, Africa, collect the skull of a colobus monkey for testing. They are part of a program sponsored by the WHO to find the source of the ebola virus. Colobus monkeys are only one suspected host. Others include bats and rodents.

When Infection Occurs

If a person becomes infected with a viral hemorrhagic fever, the local community usually takes steps to prevent the disease from spreading. This is best achieved by avoiding close physical contact with the patient and wearing appropriate protective clothing. People caring for the patient must pay close attention to their own hygiene, and disinfect or safely dispose of medical equipment after use.

Monitoring Outbreaks

Countries report outbreaks of VHFs to the World Health Organization (WHO), which analyses the information. The organization then tries to predict where new outbreaks are likely to occur. This helps governments take precautions to limit the spread of diseases. The WHO analyses a wide variety of data, including environmental factors. For example, if the food supply of rats is particularly abundant in one area, the animal is more likely to thrive, placing people in that area at greater risk for diseases carried by rats.

Into the Future

Scientists studying viral hemorrhagic fevers have several aims. Some are working on ways to prevent the spread of infections, such as improved insect control. Others hope to develop effective treatments or vaccines. Other scientists are attempting to improve methods of diagnosis. They are studying how the diseases are transmitted and how they affect the body (a study known as pathogenesis). This will help them more quickly identify these diseases in future.

Scientists studying these viruses risk becoming infected themselves. Therefore, laboratory procedures are designed to make sure the virus does not escape from the containers in which it is kept. Not all laboratories have such a secure environment. However, researchers have found a way to alter the Ebola virus so that it cannot multiply, allowing them to study it safely. Scientists hope to develop similar techniques for other viruses. Diagnosis and treatments are likely to improve as our knowledge of these diseases increases.

WHAT WOULD YOU DO?

You Are in Charge

As health minister for a country where viral hemorrhagic fevers occur regularly, you spend your money on:

■ ways to reduce human contact with the animals and insects that carry the viruses

■ developing vaccines

■ improving medication

■ improving sanitation and hygiene

Which of those methods do you think would be most effective in controlling outbreaks? Why?

CHAPTER 7

Malaria

It is 2025. Millions of people in Africa, India, and the Middle East have malaria. Supplies of medication are running dangerously low. Medical workers are swamped by new cases every day. Newspapers, billboards, radio, television, and the Internet spread antimalaria advice to as many people as possible. As summer approaches, temperatures in Mediterranean countries are rising and cases of malaria are being reported in southern Europe. People are canceling vacations to areas where malaria is a problem. The Mediterranean tourist trade is also being affected. Scientists are tracking the mosquito population to try to predict where the next outbreak will occur.

What Is Malaria?

Malaria is a disease that usually occurs in warm countries, especially Africa and Asia. In some places, the number of cases stays the same throughout the year. In other areas, the number of cases follows a seasonal pattern, with most outbreaks occurring during the rainy season. More than 500 million people become seriously ill with malaria each year. More than one million die. Children and pregnant women are at greater risk than other groups. The WHO reports that a child dies from malaria every 30 seconds. Malaria symptoms, which include fever, headache, chills, and vomiting, usually appear about 10 to 15 days after infection.

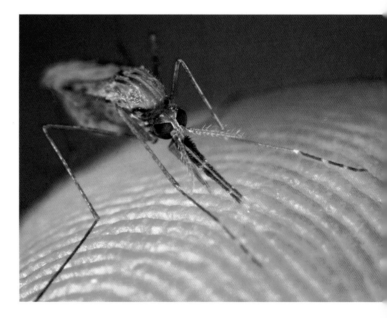

Female *Anopheles gambiae* mosquitoes like this one, which has been photographed on a human finger, transmit malaria.

What Causes Malaria?

Malaria is caused by a parasite called *Plasmodium*. There are four species of this parasite that can infect humans. One of them, *Plasmodium falciparum*, causes a far more serious illness than the others. This species is responsible for most malarial deaths.

How Does Malaria Spread?

The *Plasmodium* parasite infects people through an insect vector: the mosquito. It does not spread directly from human to human. When an infected mosquito bites a human, the mosquito transfers *Plasmodia* cells into the person's blood. The *Plasmodia* cells are carried in the blood to the liver, where they reproduce rapidly. The new *Plasmodia* cells escape back into the bloodstream and enter the red blood cells. The infected red blood cells burst, releasing *Plasmodia* cells, which further spread the infection. Red blood cells' normal function is to carry oxygen around the body. However, the infection prevents them from doing this, so the victim becomes short of oxygen. If another mosquito bites the infected person, it sucks up blood that contains *Plasmodia* cells. If that mosquito bites somebody else, it will transfer the infection to that person. As this cycle continues, more and more people become infected.

The malarial cycle involves *Plasmodia* parasites, mosquitoes, and humans. This diagram shows how the three are linked, and how the disease is spread.

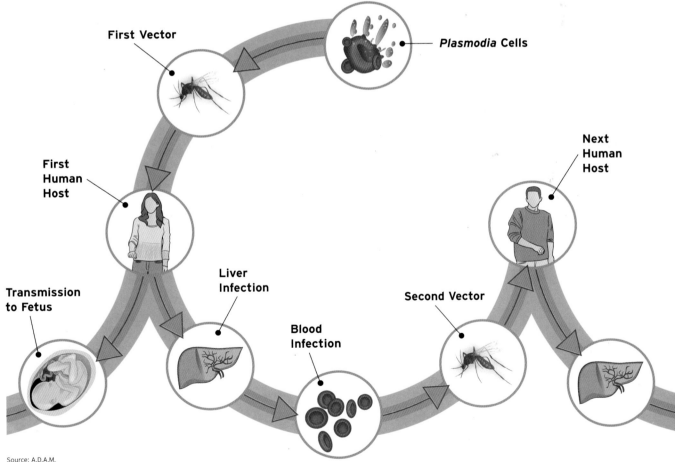

First Vector

Plasmodia Cells

First Human Host

Next Human Host

Transmission to Fetus

Liver Infection

Blood Infection

Second Vector

Source: A.D.A.M.

35

Treating Malaria

Malaria isn't a serious illness if it's diagnosed and treated early. A traditional remedy for malaria is a drug called quinine. Modern medicines, based on a chemical called artemisinin, can kill *Plasmodia* cells. However, widespread use of these medicines has created strains of drug-resistant *Plasmodia*. Despite intensive research, there are as yet no effective alternatives to artemisinin medicines for the treatment of malaria.

Avoiding Malaria

Individuals can reduce their risk of catching malaria by taking a few simple precautions. These include taking antimalarial drugs, keeping skin covered, using an insect repellent, and sleeping underneath an insecticide-treated mosquito net. Travelers to malaria-prone regions are usually able to follow these guidelines. However, people who live in such countries often lack the resources to protect themselves. An effective antimalaria vaccine is not yet available. However, scientists

A young volunteer helps a healthcare worker demonstrate the correct way to use a mosquito net in Antsokia Woreda, Ethiopia. The nets are being distributed as part of a campaign against malaria, Ethiopia's deadliest disease.

hope that one will soon be developed. One team has found a way of interfering with the reproduction of *Plasmodia* cells. Scientists hope that this discovery may lead to the development of an effective vaccine.

Controlling Malaria Outbreaks

Most efforts to control malaria involve reducing the mosquito population. Without mosquitoes, the *Plasmodia* parasites cannot infect humans. The insecticides DDT and pyrethrum are both effective against the mosquitoes. However, insecticide-resistant mosquito strains are developing. Research is continuing into other ways to control the mosquito population. One method involves introducing a natural predator such as the mosquitofish, which eats mosquitoes.

Malaria and Sickle-Cell Anemia

Sickle-cell anemia is a blood disorder. It occurs in the same parts of the world as malaria. People with sickle-cell anemia have distorted red blood cells that cannot carry oxygen efficiently. The condition is inherited, but only people who inherit a sickle-cell gene from each parent develop full sickle-cell anemia. People who inherit a single sickle-cell gene from just one parent will have a milder condition called sickle-cell trait. Scientists have found that, although sickle-cell anemia can cause serious illness, there is some benefit in having sickle-cell trait, as it offers some protection against malaria. This is because the *Plasmodia* cells cannot survive in the distorted red blood cells. Studies of people with sickle-cell trait have given scientists new insights into how the immune system can fight malaria.

WHAT WOULD YOU DO?

You Are in Charge

You run a tourism company in a country where malaria is widespread. What is your advice to people visiting your country?

- take antimalarial medication before, during, and after your trip
- use mosquito nets at night
- use insect repellent

Which of those precautions do you think would best protect tourists against malaria while increasing or maintaining tourism?

CHAPTER 8

Meningitis

It is 2025. A few weeks ago, a case of meningitis was reported in a young child who died in the hospital. Despite rapid vaccination of all the child's close contacts, within several days students from the same school also showed symptoms of the infection. More lives were lost. The vaccination program widened but it appears to have been too late. More cases are appearing. Doctors fear a major epidemic is about to grip the country. Although some cases have been seen in adults, most victims have been young children. Many parents are keeping their children at home until the crisis is over. Schools and daycare centers in badly hit areas are closing to reduce the risk of children passing the infection on to others. People hope the worst is over, but fear there may be many more deaths.

What Is Meningitis?

Meningitis is an infection of the meninges, the lining of the brain and spinal cord. There are two types: viral meningitis and bacterial meningitis. Viral meningitis is rarely serious, causing flu-like symptoms from which most people recover quickly. Bacterial meningitis is much more serious. It can cause brain damage or even death if not treated quickly. Several different bacteria can cause meningitis but *Neisseria meningitidis* (meningococcus) is the most important because it is most likely to pass from person to person.

What Are the Symptoms of Meningitis?

Meningococcal meningitis can cause symptoms within just a few hours of entering the body. The first sign is often a rash of small purple-red spots, which spread rapidly. Unlike most rashes, a meningitis rash does not fade when pressure is applied to the skin. Babies and young children often become either stiff or very floppy. They breathe rapidly and have a high fever. Older children and adults often suffer from a stiff neck, severe headache, sensitivity to light, fever, and other symptoms such as muscle cramps.

If meningitis is suspected, the patient is usually taken immediately to the hospital. The doctor removes a small amount of fluid from the patient's spine, a procedure known as a lumbar puncture. Tests on the fluid will show whether the meningococcus bacteria is present.

What Treatments Are Available?

Doctors usually give patients antibiotics as soon as possible. However, antibiotics cannot be given before the lumbar sample is taken. Killing the bacteria could give a negative diagnosis. If a small number of live bacteria survive undetected, they will multiply and the infection will worsen. To speed the treatment, medical staff deliver antibiotics directly into the bloodstream. Close monitoring of the patient's condition is essential to check that no complications develop.

What Are the Long-term Effects?

Meningococcal meningitis can be fatal. People who recover often suffer long-term effects, such as eyesight or hearing loss.

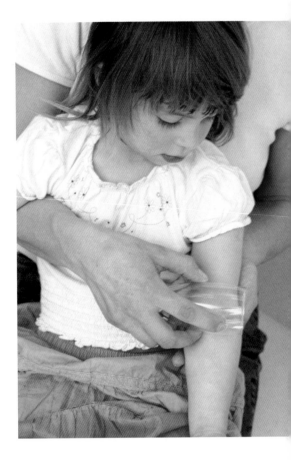

A mother tests her daughter for meningitis by pressing a clear glass against her skin. A common symptom of meningitis is a blotchy skin rash, which does not fade under pressure. If the rash does not fade, medical help should be sought immediately.

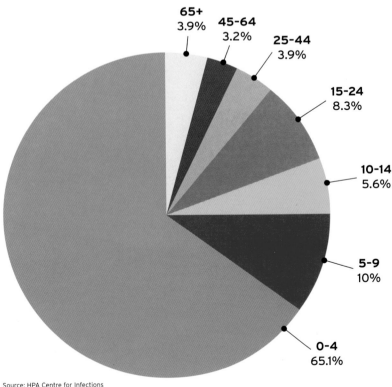

65+
3.9%
45-64
3.2%
25-44
3.9%
15-24
8.3%
10-14
5.6%
5-9
10%
0-4
65.1%

Source: HPA Centre for Infections

This pie chart shows the percentage of meningitis cases in different age groups in one year in England and Wales. Nearly two-thirds of the cases were in children under five years old.

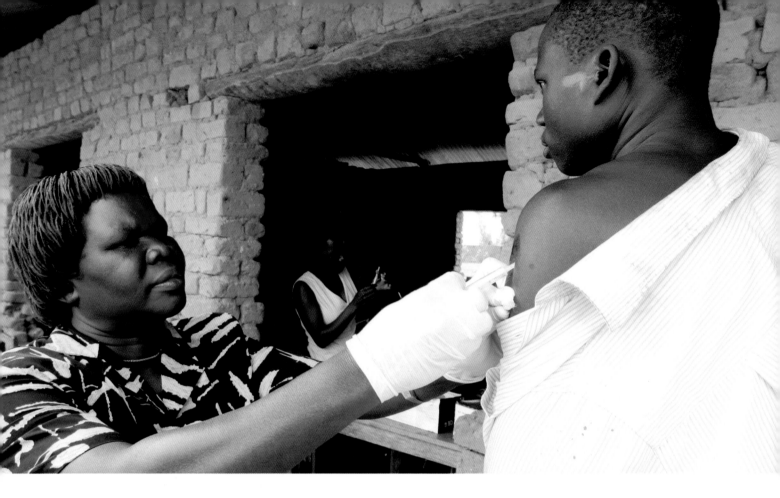

How Does Meningitis Spread?

The meningococcal bacteria pass from person to person through droplets expelled by coughing or sneezing. Being close to an infected person and sharing eating and drinking utensils increases the chance of infection. If someone becomes infected, the people who live with the victim are most at risk.

How Can the Spread of Meningitis Be Prevented or Limited?

Several actions can help reduce the spread of meningitis. These include:

- **Routine vaccination** In some countries, an entire population is vaccinated. Saudi Arabia, for example, offers routine vaccination for everyone. In Sudan and some other countries, schoolchildren are vaccinated.
- **Preventive vaccination** This can be used for people traveling to an area where there is an outbreak of meningitis.
- **Protection of close contacts** When a case of meningitis is diagnosed, people who have been in close contact with the patient need to be protected by a vaccine and antibiotics.

A medical worker injects a man with a meningitis vaccine in Uganda. In a massive campaign in 2007, more than 300,000 people in one district were vaccinated in just three weeks.

Where and When Does Meningitis Occur?

Meningococcal meningitis outbreaks occur worldwide, typically in small clusters. Most countries have reported outbreaks at some time. However, outbreaks are particularly common in poor, overcrowded areas in developing countries, especially in Africa's "meningitis belt." This region stretches from Senegal, the Gambia, and Guinea in the west, to Sudan and Ethiopia in the east.

Meningitis outbreaks also seem to be affected by the seasons. In temperate regions, such as Europe and the United States, most cases occur during winter and spring. In Africa and Asia, they are most likely to occur during the dry season between December and June.

Controlling an Epidemic

Countries prone to meningitis constantly monitor the situation to pinpoint outbreaks quickly. This enables them to give antibiotics as soon as possible. The World Health Organization (WHO) recommends mass vaccination in the region where an epidemic begins and in nearby areas. Experts estimate that if mass vaccination is carried out promptly, 70 percent of cases will be avoided.

WHAT WOULD YOU DO?

You Are in Charge
There have been a few isolated cases of meningitis in your country. You are head of public information for the government. How would you raise public awareness about the signs of meningitis and what to do if a case is suspected?

- distribute posters and flyers in hospitals, medical centers, libraries, and other public places
- broadcast information on television and radio
- print articles in newspapers and magazines
- send letters to every household
- put information on the Internet

Which do you think would be most effective? Why?

CHAPTER 9

Gone But Not Forgotten

It is 2025. A polio epidemic is sweeping through the United States, leaving people paralyzed, or in the most serious cases, dead. The first case involved a girl who came to the United States from India, where polio is still widespread. A mass vaccination program begun in 1955 had made polio rare in the United States. After decades without polio, many Americans thought their children no longer needed the vaccine. As a result, the virus is now spreading rapidly among unvaccinated children. Health officials have launched a mass vaccination campaign. They are also alerting doctors, many of whom had never seen a case of polio before. More people are being diagnosed every day. Some countries are considering quarantine restrictions on people traveling from the United States to prevent the epidemic from spreading.

How Could This Happen?

Polio, or poliomyelitis, is a viral infection that attacks the nerves and the brain. Until the 1950s, polio was common in the United States. At that time, vaccines were developed. Mass vaccination led to a rapid decrease in the number of cases of polio. By the 1970s, Americans began to view polio as a disease of the past. Like many contagious diseases, however, polio is just a plane ride away. Mass vaccination programs have eradicated diseases from some countries. But unless everyone is vaccinated, people are still at risk. Some diseases have been contained worldwide. Today, the viruses that caused them exist only in laboratories. Yet even these viruses pose a threat.

Out of the Lab

The microorganisms that cause some deadly diseases can still be found in medical facilities around the world. They are kept for research purposes. For example, because deadly bubonic plague (which wiped out a quarter of Europe's population during the Middle Ages) still occurs naturally, research into new treatments and vaccines is necessary. Therefore, a laboratory may need to use a sample of the microorganism that causes plague. Such biological materials may also be needed to research treatments for future biological weapons. These biological materials could find their way into the general population either by accident or by intention as a biological weapon.

A scientist conducts research in a laboratory with a very high level of security. He is wearing a protective suit with a helmet. His face mask is supplied with air via overhead lines that plug into the suit.

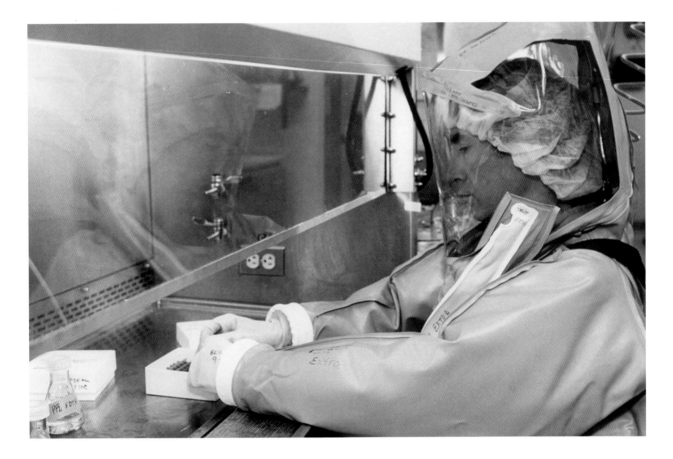

MINIMIZING LABORATORY RISKS

There is always a small chance that dangerous, infectious biological material might get out of a laboratory and cause an epidemic or pandemic. To minimize this risk, laboratories need to maintain high standards of safety and security. Laboratories follow safety guidelines to minimize the risk of dangerous material escaping. Official inspections ensure that people take safety precautions. These include using a filtered ventilation system, working in biological safety cabinets, and wearing protective clothing. Tight laboratory security is also maintained to reduce the possibility of any dangerous material being stolen.

Eradicating Infectious Diseases

In an ideal world, infectious diseases would not exist. This may not be achievable, but there are worldwide programs in place to eradicate (wipe out) individual diseases. The World Health Organization began a program to eradicate smallpox in 1967. The last case of smallpox was reported in 1977. The WHO declared the disease officially eradicated in 1980. Diseases spread in many different ways. That means scientists need to use different approaches to eradicate them. For some diseases, developing a vaccine is the best solution. Other diseases can be controlled and eliminated by improving sanitation and hygiene.

SOME INFECTIOUS DISEASES AND THEIR CHANCES OF ERADICATION

Disease	Possible Obstacles	Eradicable?
Polio	technically possible; needs greater national/international commitment	yes
Guinea worm disease	lack of awareness; inadequate funding to make water supplies safe	yes
Pork tapeworm	need better diagnostic tests for humans and pigs	potentially
Hepatitis B	some people are carriers; cannot prevent infection of baby before birth; infant vaccination needed	not at present, but could be reduced over time
Rabies	vaccines effective on pets but can't vaccinate all wild animals	no, but could be eliminated in towns and cities

Success Story

Polio is an example of significant success in the battle against an infectious disease. It is now very rare for a case of polio to appear in the industrialized world. However, the disease is still endemic in Nigeria, Afghanistan, India, and Pakistan. In 1988, the Global Polio Eradication Initiative was launched. Children around the world were vaccinated. As a result, the incidence of polio has decreased from 350,000 cases per year in 1988 to just 1,313 in 2007. Scientists hope that further vaccination programs will eradicate the disease completely. Vigilance is necessary, though. Somalia, declared polio-free in 2002, became reinfected from Nigeria in 2005. However, the last case was reported in 2007. In 2008, the country was again declared polio-free.

Scientists and health experts are convinced that some other deadly infectious diseases could be eradicated, too. However, international commitment and cooperation, together with adequate funding, are essential if this is to be achieved.

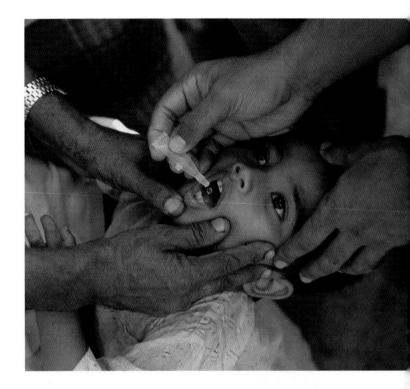

Just two drops of polio vaccine will protect this Bangladeshi boy from a virus that once crippled millions of children. Global efforts have nearly eradicated polio.

WHAT WOULD YOU DO?

You Are in Charge

You run the government's vaccination program. Many people think they do not need vaccines for diseases that are no longer a problem in your country. Others worry about the safety of vaccines. You know how easily diseases spread from one country to the next. You also know that vaccines are safe and effective ways to prevent diseases from spreading. How do you convince people to get vaccinated?

■ You develop a public awareness campaign about vaccine safety and the importance of vaccinations.

■ You make sure every doctor has information about vaccine safety to hand out to patients.

■ You require that all children be vaccinated before they are allowed to attend school.

Which of those options would be the most effective way to persuade people to get vaccinated? Why?

Glossary

abstinence To refrain from doing something

antibiotic A medicine used to treat bacterial infections

antibody A protein produced by white blood cells in response to the presence of a bacterium or virus

antiviral A medicine used to treat viral infections

bacteria A type of microorganism that can reproduce independently

cell One of the tiny units of which all living things are made

cesarean section A surgical procedure that can be used to deliver a child

contagious Transmitted from one person to another by direct contact

cull To kill part of an animal population, for example, to prevent an epidemic

diagnose To identify an illness or disorder

domesticated Cultivated, raised, or bred for human companionship or consumption

endemic Occurring naturally in a particular place

epidemic An outbreak of an infectious disease that affects many people

eradicate To completely destroy something so that it is unable to recur

fungi A type of microorganism that reproduces by spores and lives by absorbing nutrients from organic matter

genetic To do with passing biological information from one generation to the next

host An organism that a microorganism infects, such as a human or animal

hygiene Health and cleanliness

immune system The body's defense against infection and other illnesses

immunity Resistance to infection

infectious Describing something that can spread from person to person

inherited Passed from one generation to the next

microorganism An organism that is too small to be seen with the naked eye

mutate To undergo a genetic change, resulting in a new characteristic

pandemic An outbreak of an infection affecting many people over a large area

parasite An organism that lives on or in another (host) organism in a way that harms or is of no advantage to the host

primate A member of the order of mammals that includes humans, apes, and monkeys

quarantine Keep away from others to prevent the spread of infection

refugee Someone who seeks refuge, especially from war or persecution, by going to a foreign country

sanitation Maintenance of public health and hygiene, especially the water supply and sewage systems

spore The reproductive structure of some microorganisms

sterile Free from living bacteria or other microorganisms

strain A subgroup of a species of organism

Sub-Saharan Africa The region of Africa that lies south of the Sahara; it includes the countries of east, central, west, and southern Africa

surveillance Continual observation

symptom An indication of an illness

transfusion The process of giving a patient blood from another person

transmission Passing from one person or thing to another

vaccine A substance used to produce immunity from a particular infection

vector An organism, such as a mosquito, that transmits disease-causing microorganisms from infected individuals to other people, or from infected animals to human beings

veterinary To do with diseases of animals and their treatment

virus A type of microorganism that cannot reproduce independently

World Health Organization (WHO) An agency of the United Nations that coordinates international efforts to fight disease and promote health

Further Information

Books

Haugen, David. *Pandemics* At Issue (series). (Greenhaven Press, 2007)

Hoff, Brent and Carter Smith. *Mapping Epidemics: A Historical Atlas of Disease* (Franklin Watts, 2006)

Kramer, Ann. *Epidemics* In the News (series). (Franklin Watts, 2007)

Walker, Richard. *Epidemics and Plagues.* Kingfisher Knowledge (series). (Kingfisher Publishing, 2006)

Weinman, Sarah. *Pandemics: Epidemics in a Shrinking World* In the News (series). (Rosen Publishing, 2007)

Williams, Mary (editor). *Epidemics.* Opposing Viewpoints (series). (Greenhaven Publishing, 2005)

Web Sites

American Museum of Natural History
Epidemic! The World of Infectious Disease
www.amnh.org/exhibition/epidemic

Check out the companion web site to the exhibit that includes articles, images, a suggested reading list, and glossary terms.

Centers for Disease Control and Prevention
www.cdc.gov/ncidod/SARS

Read basic facts and frequently asked questions about the 2003 SARS outbreak and examine plans to control the disease in the future.

U.S. National Archives and Records
www.archives.gov/exhibits/influenza-epidemic

View interesting primary source photographs and documents that tell the story of the deadly U.S. influenza epidemic of 1918–1919.

World Health Organization
www.who.int/csr/disease/avian_influenza/en

Get updated facts and information about avian influenza and the efforts to track its development around the world.

What Would You Do?

Page 7:
If information about diagnosed cases of infectious disease is collected centrally, it can be analyzed regularly. This should allow authorities to spot trends and provide an early warning of a developing epidemic. Detailed information about the location, age, gender, ethnic group, and recent travels of those infected can help to build a more complete picture of what is happening. All of this data would be helpful in monitoring the outbreak of an epidemic.

Page 13:
Education about how to avoid infection should, if people follow the advice, reduce the number of new cases of HIV. Available medicines for treating HIV/AIDS are very expensive and active steps to achieve a reduction in their cost would benefit many. An effective vaccine would protect those not yet infected but would be of no benefit to existing sufferers. For a developing country, spending on scientific research would be a low-priority, as this would be better done in well-funded laboratories in the industrialized world. It is probably more important for a developing country to spend money on education and buying drugs to keep people alive.

Page 21:
Key workers include medical staff who would help anyone who became ill. It would therefore be sensible to vaccinate these people first. After that, the most vulnerable people, such as children and older adults, would be in greatest need of protection. Most people think it's unfair to vaccinate those who could pay while leaving the poor at risk. Others might think it is unfair to vaccinate people on a random first come, first-served basis.

Page 25:
Banning all travel into and out of the country could have a disastrous economic effect, as well as disrupting supplies of food and other essentials. Banning travel to and from SARS-affected regions, while at the same time quarantining arrivals from other areas, would greatly reduce the risk of a SARS outbreak in the country. However, this would be very costly and may prove impractical. Screening arrivals may be the only viable option – even if it would not prevent the possibility of a SARS outbreak.

Page 29:
Controlling antibiotic use in humans and animals could slow down the development of new antibiotic-resistant strains. Improving hospital hygiene would also help reduce infections. Testing and quarantining patients would also prevent the spread of infection. Each of those tactics has a part to play in reducing

the incidence of antibiotic-resistant infections. Developing new antibiotics would offer treatment against those resistant strains that already exist, but would probably result in the appearance of even more resistant strains.

Page 33:
Without the animal or insect host, microorganisms cannot infect humans, so vector control plays a big part in helping to reduce infections. Effective vaccines would help to prevent future infections, while improved medication would reduce the severity of infections. Although poor communities would generally benefit from improved sanitation and hygiene, this would only help control those infections where lack of sanitation played a part in transmission.

Page 37:
Advising people not to visit your country would be disastrous for your business. It would also affect the economy as a whole and cause unemployment for many people. Travelers could be encouraged to visit, provided they heed the advice about antimalarial medication, mosquito nets, and insect repellent.

Page 41:
Think about where you, your friends, and family would be most likely to access such information. Do you take any notice of posters and flyers in public places? Do you get information from television and radio, or are you more likely to read newspapers or web sites? How much do you think it would cost to send letters to every household – and would you read them if you received them? Thinking about where you get your information from can help you decide on effective ways of reaching the population as a whole.

Page 45:
If people understood more about the dangers of some infectious diseases, vaccine safety, and the importance of vaccinations, they might be persuaded to get vaccinated. Raising public awareness about these issues could therefore be an effective way of achieving your goal. Providing pamphlets for doctors to hand out would be a good way of making sure people had accurate information, but would only reach those people who had visited a doctor. You would still need to find ways to reach the rest of the population. Making vaccination mandatory for all children would certainly increase the numbers vaccinated, although there is a good chance that some people would object to a mandatory vaccination.

Index

Page numbers in **bold** refer to illustrations and charts.

About the Author
Dr. Carol Ballard worked for many years as a school science coordinator. She is now a full-time writer of books for children and teenagers. Her books include *Fighting Infectious Diseases*.